DANCING INTO OPPORTUNITY™

The Rhythm of Effective Communication

MIGDALIA GONZALEZ

DANCING INTO OPPORTUNITY™

It is sold with the understanding that the publisher and the individual authors are not engaged in the rendering of psychological, legal, accounting or other professional advice. The content and views in each chapter are the sole expression and opinion of its author and not necessarily the views of Fig Factor Media, LLC.

Published by
Fig Factor Media, LLC | www.figfactormedia.com

Cover & Layout Design by
Marco Antonio Álvarez Rodríguez

Printed in the United States of America

ISBN: 978-1-957058-80-1
Library of Congress Number: 2025915249

FIG
FACTOR
MEDIA

DANCING INTO OPPORTUNITY™

DANCING INTO OPPORTUNITY™

This book is dedicated to my cheerleaders: my son, JMN, who left this world too early and suggested I write this book; my daughter, JAN, who continues to dream, and share her talent with others; and my biggest cheerleader RP who always believes in me. To all the dancers of the world—the dreamers, the closet dancers, and to all the professionals who grace us with their talent—keep dancing.

TABLE OF CONTENTS

PREFACE

"A Dance of Legacy and Love"

When I first opened *Dancing into Opportunity*, I didn't just read Migdalia's words, I felt them. I heard the music of her ancestors, saw the flash of her abuela's joy in the kitchen, and sensed the tender ache of promises made and kept through grief. This is not just a book about communication; it is a memoir in motion, a tribute to legacy, to love, and to all the ways our stories dance before we even know the steps.

There's a moment in life when words spoken by someone we love become a mission, a calling. Migdalia's son, JMN, gifted her such a moment. He saw her light, her wisdom, and encouraged her to share it. And she did, with her whole heart.

In *Dancing into Opportunity*, Migdalia brings forward her truth with candor, clarity, and care. She teaches us that communication is not just about speaking or listening; it's about harmonizing. It's about meeting people where they are, honoring where they've been, and co-creating where we are going.

Migdalia has written a guide, yes, but more than that, she's created an invitation. To feel, to listen, to move toward one another with empathy and grace. Her metaphor of dance as communication is profound. It reflects everything I believe about leadership, relationships, and how we transform spaces and people—through presence, rhythm, care, and vulnerability.

As someone who believes deeply in creating more compassionate, cohesive, and collaborative leaders, partnerships, teams, cultures, and society, I see this book as an anthem for humanity. It's a resource, a reflection, and a revelation to guide us in workplaces and in our everyday lives. Migdalia, thank you for keeping your promise. You've given the world a gift. Your son's whisper is now a legacy that will ripple into countless lives.

I know her story will stir something deep within you. Let it. Let it remind you that we are all learning new steps each day and that with open hearts, we can dance into every opportunity with courage, gratitude, and love.

Mali Phonpadith

Founder & CEO, SOAR Community Network
TEDx Speaker, Bestselling Author

INTRODUCTION

The idea for this book was born in a moment I will never forget. I just delivered a presentation on effective communications, something I have spoken about countless times—but this day was different. My college son attended the session with me. I would sometimes force my kids to volunteer at events I participated in. My goal was to give them exposure to the business world. In this session, I introduced a new concept—dancing into opportunity.

As I addressed the group, filled with people from all walks of life, I paused and said, "Effective communication is like a dance." The words caught in the air and settled with weight. I went on to explain that every interaction, whether with one person or a group, is like learning a new dance. You have to figure out how the other person dances (communicates), sense their rhythm, understand their steps, and respect their space. You must be willing to move in harmony with others who come from different backgrounds, cultures, and life experiences. It is not always easy. Sometimes you lead, sometimes you follow. But when you are attuned, something beautiful happens—real communication flows.

My son, JMN, listened, smiled, and later said to me, "Mom, you should write a book about that." He made me promise. I smiled, enjoying the few moments when your teenager thinks you are "cool" ... not knowing at the time how deeply those words would stay with me.

My son is no longer with us.

This book is my dance with grief, love, memory, and a promise fulfilled. Dance and music are the soul's memory—carrying the echoes of love, the joy of special moments, and the silent presence of those we have lost. In every rhythm and every step, we are reminded that while time moves on, the beauty of those memories dance within us forever. My daughter reminded me of the book; my hubby encouraged me to write it; my "board" of support (my tribe know who they are), and my grandson, DAR, for inspiration. I wrote it for those who want to connect more deeply, speak more clearly, and build more meaningful relationships through the power of communication.

So, here it is: *Dancing into Opportunity*.

— Migdalia

I will be open, present, vulnerable, attentive to the dance of opportunity, and learn to dance, to soar into the best version of me to facilitate others to be the best version of themselves.

I. SET THE STAGE

In the grand ballroom of human connection, every relationship, transaction, or endeavor begins with a dance. Whether it is the subtle sway of body language in conversation, the carefully timed give-and-take of negotiation, or the intuitive rhythm of collaboration, success depends not merely on the steps taken but, on the commitment, to move with purpose toward a shared goal. Dance, as both metaphor and method, reveals that meaningful engagement requires more than skill—it demands presence, responsiveness, and an unspoken promise to follow through. This book invites you to explore how the principles of dance can set the stage for authentic, intentional relationships in every area of life and setting the stage is just the beginning.

Throughout history, dance has served as a powerful form of storytelling, expression, and connection. From ancient rituals and tribal ceremonies to classical ballets and modern street performances, dance has communicated emotions, preserved cultural traditions, and marked momentous events in people's lives. It transcends language, allowing people to share their experiences and values through movement. Across time and cultures, dance has brought communities together—celebrating unity, identity, and the universal human desire to connect through rhythm and motion.

I love dancing. I mean, I really love dancing. I enjoy the entire process from start to finish. Watching dancers perform their routines, whether in a group or as soloists, the energy expressed through their movements. Discovering the steps and the story behind the dance is fascinating. Coordinating steps and movements, with music or not, conveys a message, a feeling, and a vibe to tell a story can be highly effective. Dance, especially when paired with music, serves as a powerful means of connection and communication. It incorporates rhythm and culture into relationship-building in a unique way.

Effective communication is not just about the words we use. It is a combination of our words and how we move to convey those messages. Our bodies become instruments of expression, often speaking louder than our voices, revealing intent, emotion, and connection long before a single word is said. Body language plays a crucial role in expressing our thoughts, emotions, and intentions through gestures, facial expressions, posture, and eye contact. We can communicate feelings such as confidence, sincerity, or empathy. For instance, a smile can indicate friendliness, while crossed arms might suggest anger or defensiveness. By being aware of our body language and interpreting others' non-verbal cues, we can enhance our interactions and build strong relationships. But this is only the beginning of using effective communications to build relationships. However, to avoid misunderstandings, it is essential to understand who you are dealing with. Learning about others is essential for effective interaction. Building relationships with new acquaintances, colleagues, or teammates requires effort and it is crucial to learn who you are dealing with to effectively dance with them. Each interaction requires effort, strategic, precise steps to convey a message which can enhance or detract from your performance. It is all a dance.

Just as every dance movement is shaped by the music that surrounds it, our ability to communicate is tied to the rhythms and melodies of our own experiences. The interplay of movement and sound creates an environment where connection flourishes— each gesture, pause, or step creates a deeper meaning when guided by the pulse of music. It is in this harmonious blending of dance and music that we find the most profound opportunities for understanding and expression.

Music is one of the oldest and most enduring forms of human expression, woven into the fabric of every culture throughout history. It transcends language, bringing people together across time, place, and difference. With a few notes, it can stir deep emotions, awaken forgotten memories, and remind us of those we have loved and lost. Music has the power to move us—not only in feeling, but in action—uniting crowds in protest, celebration, and shared humanity. It echoes through our most joyful moments and comforts us in our sorrow, a timeless thread connecting heart to heart. Music and dance are inseparable. Together, they create vivid experiences that evoke emotions and memories. They can take you to places you can only imagine, make you feel certain things or revive precious memories. Music and dance hold unique meanings for different people and enhance any performance.

There are genres that are not on my top ten, but they all have their own merits. One significant lesson I emphasize when mentoring others is to recognize that not every individual or situation will align with your preferences. However, it is possible to learn to appreciate the value they bring. To create and establish great relationships you must learn to communicate or "dance" with others. This is a vital key to your own success. This is a fact. No matter how hard you try to make someone like you, you cannot, but what you can do is learn to effectively communicate or "dance" with others who are different then you. It is important to remember that everyone has unique experiences and memories that influence their ways of communication.

As far back as I can remember, I heard music, laughter, and saw people dancing around me. Family gatherings were filled with music, dancing, and food, always together. I grew up in a family, where we may not have been rich, but we celebrated together always. Family was a constant force around me. I was the first baby in the family, and my aunts were my babysitters. They always played music, and I genuinely believe it was their influence and their love of music that set the stage for my love affair with music. My mom and her siblings were the first generation born in Puerto Rico but raised in New York. Our home balanced Puerto Rican traditions with American influences in everything we did— celebrations, food, and music. Sometimes it worked, sometimes it did not. Everyone has had to balance a new job, relationship, environment, or customs. Success comes from building a foundation that combines your experiences and teachings, enabling personal and professional growth.

I can close my eyes and remember walking through the old railroad style apartment connecting one room to another. I knew who was in what room because of the music that was playing. One room had rock & roll, another had Spanish music, but when I headed straight to the kitchen that is where I could hear my favorite voice, my abuela singing a ballad from the likes of Tito Rodriguez or Los Panchos. During my early years, I would hear my abuela humming and singing while she was cooking. Abuela, for those who do not speak Spanish, means grandmother; her name was Carmen Lugo. I swear she was a magician. She raised six children, buried her first-born, and came to the states without speaking English, no education, and a single mom. She did her best raising her six kids on a seamstress salary, worked factories, did whatever she had to do to make sure there was food on the table. She was a community activist and an entrepreneur. In today's terms, she was a boss lady, a real hustler.

She was a determined, resourceful woman who could sew a beautiful dress from scraps, quickly serve a fresh cup of coffee, and prepare a plate of food in a matter of minutes. There was always food on the table, with a little extra *por si acaso*, just in case someone showed up. Food was her love language. I could close my eyes and hear her humming, "En Mi Viejo San Juan," a song that has symbolically become an anthem for many Puerto Ricans who migrated to the States for a better life. The singer talks about the dreams and memories of growing up in Puerto Rico and that one day he will return. Almost every Puerto Rican knows the song and can sing or hum it at the drop of a dime. A perfect example of the impact and power of a song and its words.

Your memories and experiences affect and influence how you will interact with others. Just like in music and dance, harmony and rhythm come from understanding your partner— knowing their tempo, their style, and where they want to go. In any collaboration, doing your own research is essential. Taking the time to learn about the other person's goals, values, and vision helps you find the common beat between you. It allows you to spot connections, align intentions, and build trust. Whether you are stepping into a duet or joining a larger ensemble, this groundwork sets the stage for working together with flow, respect, and shared purpose.

Effective communication requires practice and vulnerability. Being open to learning, willing to fail initially, and committed to mastering skills can foster meaningful relationships. Embrace transparency, responsibility, and accountability to deliver clear messages with purpose. Aim to create an inclusive environment that welcomes diverse thoughts, opinions, beliefs, and cultures.

Feet together.
Using left leg take a step to the left, right leg step right.
Step 1 (left), Step 2 (right), now repeat. Step 1, Step 2... Step 1, Step 2...
Now together.

1, 2... 1, 2... 1, 2... 1, 2.

II. DANCE

Dance is a tightrope—a delicate balancing act many have experienced. Learning something new, adapting to unfamiliar surroundings, navigating new paths of life, while holding on to the values and traditions that shape who you are. It is the constant shift between worlds: honoring where we come from while embracing where we are. For immigrants and migrants, this experience is not just a moment, but a continuous journey—one of courage, resilience, and identity. It is a common story, built on hope and hard choices, reminding us that the path forward often requires us to take a step even when it is uncomfortable. It is essential to cultivate comfort in situations of discomfort, which requires the willingness to start engagement with others. We have all had to learn how to dance through different worlds.

My grandmother insisted that I learn Spanish. Speaking both languages has opened my world to music written in other languages, expanding my music interest to more international sounds. She would often say, "You have to learn how to dance through every situation." I did not understand it when I was young, but now it makes perfect sense. Every situation you face will dictate how you will respond or dance to it. Every situation will require you to learn to adjust, assess, standstill, or face the situation head on. Your response or reaction will determine how you will dance through it all. My story is not an uncommon one;

we all experience good and tough times, unexpected changes, new jobs, and new people. We will all encounter opportunities that will either allow space for us to rise or fall to the challenge.

Embracing new opportunities is like learning an unfamiliar dance. Just as a dancer must be open to rhythms and movements, we too must be willing to step out of our comfort zones and explore uncharted territories. Each opportunity is a chance to learn, grow, and adapt, like mastering a new dance routine.

Having a global mindset is like dancing with partners from around the world. It requires understanding and appreciation of diverse perspectives, cultures, and ideas. By doing so, we can create a harmonious and dynamic performance that transcends boundaries and enriches our experiences. As a member of Generation X, I witnessed the emergence of various music genres and music videos. One notable collaboration was between one of the first rap groups and one of the prominent rock & roll bands of that time. Another significant collaboration was between a renowned jazz musician and a famous Latino timbalero, which resulted in a celebrated jazz album.

The concept is not original, mix different things together and see what happens. It is like my first time trying shrimp and grits when I moved to North Carolina. I had no idea what it was. I could not mentally process shrimp and grits. See, grits meant breakfast; we make a sweet version—sugar, vanilla, butter. So, the visual was not processing seafood and breakfast? My colleagues at work all talked about how good it was, but still my head was not having it. And then it happened. I tried it, cautiously at first, but OMG it was delicious; it has become one of my favorite plates of food. But any good southerner will tell you, it all depends on who makes it. Not everyone's hands are made for cooking (sorry, not sorry).

In my younger years, I never missed the Saturday shows that had dancers and live performances by the singers or bands of the time. My two younger aunts and I would replicate the dances we saw on TV. We learned dances like the mashed potato, twist, hustle, electric slide, line dancing, and salsa. We practiced various dance steps; some steps were easier and some were not. Dancing provided a common activity that everyone could participate in. It served as a way for individuals to connect. It was my attempt to fit in with the "cool" crowd. Dance involves multiple factors: it involves how you respond to music, what memories come to mind, and making you feel part of something bigger than you. I cannot remember when I started dancing because all I remember is that I always danced.

Music was the bridge to both worlds. It was the vehicle we used to make new friends. It gave us something to talk about with others. If you were older, it was the way you flirted with a pretty girl or a handsome man. If you were more mature, it served as a reminder of all the good times growing up. All the birthday parties, weddings, holidays, or special moments, music and dancing have always played a vital role in our lives. It does not matter where you come from, what language you speak or how old you are. We can all probably remember a dance or a song that reminds us of a special moment in time.

If you do research on the internet, the average time to catch someone's attention is between 7 to 10 seconds. In this world of technology—cell phones, computers, and other gadgets—with the abundance of information and continuous flow, effective communication has become increasingly important. It is extremely challenging to rely on texts and social media "likes" as the communication methods of preference. Technology has diminished our social skills and increased our fears of real interaction. Yet, communicating is also simple: just pause, put the gadgets down, and commit to the moment. Be present, learn a new step and dance like no one is watching because at the end of the day we only have one life. Every action has a reaction, good or bad. What you do makes a difference, even if we often do not think so. How you do it is your signature dance. What you must decide is what kind of impact do you want to have? What is the legacy you want to leave behind?

The skills used during any type of communication interaction are like the steps of a dance routine, a series of steps and moves that you have put together to be successful when interacting with others. Every dance will be different because every situation will be different. Just think about the variety of dance styles or genres. It could be traditional, like ballet, or the waltz, or it could be modern, freestyle, breakdancing, or jazz, and within each of those dance groups there are also specific styles.

Think of dancing and music as channels of communication that cross boundaries, cultures, and languages. It is the use of your body in a rhythmic way to deliver or evoke a message. A dance can be performed to music, words, or silence. It is an art form, and we all have different interpretations of what art is. It can translate a historical story, describe a folkloric event, or bring a cultural story to life. The collection of steps is a choreography of these movements with the sole purpose of expressing an idea, emotion, or just releasing energy.

Effective communication can be verbal or non-verbal steps you use to deliver your message or intent. Dance is similar because it involves both your steps and the music to deliver the performance. Mastering this skill takes practice, understanding your steps, knowing your audience, being flexible, and executing effectively. It is a skill that requires practice, a lot of practice. Every interaction involves some form of communication; every move, every step, every word is part of the interaction between you and another person. Effective communication is a series of moving parts when used together to help, support, or directly affect your message. The ability to understand and interpret your own emotions, and those of others requires practice. Learning to effectively communicate, engage, listen, and interact effectively is like a dance—with the goal of executing successful communication. You want a successful performance. You want to SHINE!

A great dance performance can evoke a wide range of emotions, from awe to joy. It may leave you in tears or prompt a standing ovation because the performance was so powerful. Dance is amazing because it communicates without words. Performers must convey their intent through movements, like our daily interactions requiring clear expression without words. Your body language, movements, voice, and tone all communicate.

The dance you put together can be compared to how you effectively communicate with others. Each communication interaction, whether a meeting at work, a discussion with your significant other, or when delivering a speech, will require you to execute moves for that situation. You begin to dance in the moment. Do I step back, slide to the right, slide to the left? What steps will you need to dance with the other person? Each situation will be different because we are all different. Whether it is classical ballet, contemporary dance, or breakdancing, each dance form offers its own unique aesthetic. Each step may seem insignificant in isolation, yet when combined, they collectively compose a striking artistic expression. Nothing is wrong with any of them alone, but when put together powerful.

Successful communication is like a well-choreographed dance, where each step contributes to a harmonious and effective interaction. It involves a combination of verbal and non-verbal cues, active listening, empathy, and clarity. To build effective relationships, it is essential to be present and attentive, ensuring that your body language, tone, and words align with intent. The skill of active listening is crucial, and it shows respect and understanding, fostering trust and openness. Empathy allows you to connect on a deeper level, acknowledging and validating the other person's feelings and perspectives.

Clarity in your message helps avoid misunderstandings and ensures that your intentions are clear. By integrating these elements, you can create meaningful and lasting relationships built on trust, respect, and mutual understanding. Many of us have experienced speaking with someone who is distracted by their phone or computer. It feels like you are being ignored, like you are not important, or translate that body language as dismissive. We are all guilty of doing that, not with bad intentions, but we all need to remember that when you are dealing with others, put the technology down.

Each situation is not only different but the circumstances surrounding that event are different, meaning there are multiple moving parts for every transaction. Effective communication requires mindfulness and adaptability, especially as each situation brings a unique set of factors. While you are the common denominator in every interaction, it is important to recognize that in each scenario the people involved will be different, with different perspectives, goals, and communication styles. Therefore, the desired outcomes will vary. To navigate this successfully, you must be intentional about assessing the environment, understanding others' motivations, and finding what approach will work for that person and situation. It is much like a dance—each partner brings their own rhythm, and your ability to adjust, respond, and move in sync will determine how well the interaction flows.

Mastering effective communication is like becoming a skilled dancer; it requires self-awareness, keen observation, and the flexibility to adapt to changing rhythms. A dancer must be in tune with their own body while staying aware of a partner and the music; a good communicator must understand their own emotions, listen closely to others, and respond with intention. This combination creates an environment where connections flow, misunderstandings are minimal, and growth becomes possible. Like dancing, communication is fluid; when you move with awareness and grace, you invite others to join in step and grow together.

You will need to identify the moves you need to effectively deliver your message. It may be the same two people having a conversation, but there may be outside circumstances that can alter the actual event. For example, your boss just gave you instructions different from the original ones she provided in your last meeting. Now there is doubt, hesitation. You are not sure what step you should take next.

As you practice your steps they become second nature. As

you become proficient in mastering these steps, you develop a unique interpretation of the dance. Even when part of a group where all members perform identical movements, each dancer contributes their own distinctive style to the performance. You learn the basics, add your own moves, and become confident in your execution of those steps.

But what happens when someone throws a wrench into your routine? They want to change a step in the process. They were not part of the planning, or the group. You have executed on the previous instructions, you thought you were on track and your boss decides to change plans without letting you know. Now you are upset and frustrated; your boss is clueless, but you still must perform. Sound familiar? You could replace the character with a spouse, a friend, a child. It does not matter; the situation is always the same. A new situation, no clarity, no direction, but the goal is the same. That is why flexibility is so vital to your success. You must pause, assess the situation, ask questions, adjust your current steps, and execute your new moves because, at the end of the day, you must find common ground, so you are all dancing together to achieve the goals.

Same project, different tasks, but now emotions are involved because there was no clarity. Learning how to be flexible and deliver your message and dance with someone is critical to finding a balance in the give and take of any interaction. Effective communication is extremely important and vital in the world we live in. As our worlds change, we must find effective steps that help us set the stage for action even when things change. It is not just about the steps; it is about mastering your own steps to create a foundation where you can leap from. For clarification, the goal should always be to build long-term relationships, not just a one-time transaction, but relationships that will be helpful in the future. People will always remember how you treated them. We are all human, not machines. We do not live in this world alone. We need and thrive on our interactions with others.

However, it is essential to find a method of communication that allows you to effectively express your sentiments, reach common ground, ensuring a collaborative effort towards achieving the goals. Though you are working on the same project with different tasks, emotions have heightened due to a lack of clarity. Learning how to stay calm, adapt, convey your message appropriately, and collaborate with others is crucial for maintaining balance in communication events.

Now that I have repeatedly expressed the importance of effective communication, how vital it is to listen, speak clearly, read the non-verbal cues, and align your intentions with your words—the world, as it often does, decides to throw a wrench into it all. Just when you think you got this communication thing down, you found your rhythm and you mastered your steps, an unexpected change in tempo forces a sudden adjustment.

Technology, we use it every day—at home, at work. It has systematically changed how we communicate with each other. The "old" way of talking face-to-face has morphed into a virtual environment, which adds another layer of complexity to how we communicate with one another. The world extends beyond our immediate surroundings and is increasingly interconnected, requiring individuals to continually adapt their approaches to communicate effectively with others. Whether at work or in our personal lives we are faced with multiple opportunities to communicate. The goal for all of us is to strategically identify the best way to express and share what we need, want, ideas, concerns, or emotions. Sometimes, we fail to realize that every moment we interact with others is a communication event. Good or bad, we are communicating with someone else—a colleague, a boss, a loved one, a child, or even a pet. What we say, how we say it, and how we use our bodies to deliver a message is integral in the execution and can determine whether your message met its mark.

Just like in dance, the more you practice your steps, the more natural and confident your movements become—and the same holds true for effective communication. When you practice your communication skills occasionally, your conversation will feel stiff, or below average, like not practicing the choreography for the performance. But as you increase your practice—whether it is active listening, clear delivery, or reading the room—your rhythm improves. With consistent, intentional practice, communicating will become fluid and instinctive. When you practice the steps, you do not have to think through every move; your body knows the steps. Once you have mastered the movements, your style comes through. Your style becomes a dance you lead with grace and ease, no matter what the tempo or partner.

I remember during a performance, we practiced all year, we were on the stage—ready, confident to perform. We were so excited because it was a fun dance routine and then it happened— the music would not start. We were all on stage in our positions and nothing happened, zilch, nada, not a sound, and one of the dancers improvised and we all stepped in until the music came on. It was just seconds, but it felt like it was forever. It could have really thrown all of us off but instead we showed flexibility to ensure the audience did not know what happened. The audience enjoyed the performance and never knew until we spoke about it.

During the first rehearsal, our teacher would explain the dance, the music, and the why behind it. As each week passed, she added or adjusted the steps until we learned the entire choreography. The steps, the moves, and, most important, the emotions behind them. We practiced them weekly for hours at a time, and when it was the week of the performance, the practice became daily. We made sure we stayed in our formation, executed our steps precisely as we practiced. Even when we were tired—emotionally and physically—we had to perform. We double-checked our alignments and our spacing with our partners in the dance until it was flawless.

I can hear the dance teacher now, "backs straight, heads up, open your arms, smile" and we practiced those steps for hours on end. Yes, it was tiring, and, yes, one of us would forget a step and we would have to start from the beginning. And, yes, we would get frustrated because sometimes, a step does not come easy. You keep practicing until one day it clicks. The day of the performance, we arrived early, some of us would not eat because of nerves, but we were so excited to perform that our energy was at 100.

When you think about it, the instructions the teacher would tell us—back's straight, heads up, open your arms, and most important smile—are basic building blocks for how we should always carry ourselves. How you present yourself to the world is the moment where others begin their assessment of you. We all do it. We step into a room, we scan the room, look for people we know or can connect with. Someone to help us balance our emotions, manage our fears, and feel supported. Even our parents have taught us to stand straight, keep your head up, and smile. My mom, and especially my grandmother, would say you must always put your best foot forward. Rich or poor does not excuse presenting yourself to the best of your ability. You must be clean, your clothes neat. How we carry ourselves, how we face the world every day is the first thing people see. This non-verbal form of communication is crucial to our success when communicating with others.

Actions speak louder than words, and even the most skilled orator can destroy his or her message if the actions do not match. People are visual animals. Our eyes quickly develop a map in our mind of how we are going to "perform" in the room. Do we know someone in the room? Is there someone you do not like? Is there anyone who can be an ally? Is there someone with whom we can connect? It is a natural process to assess "the room." Are we safe? Do I need to prepare for a conflict? Our survival response of fight, flight, or freeze is a natural response that occurs when we feel stressed, threatened, or anxious. This physiological theory describes how the body reacts to a threat. A natural response to protect ourselves. It happens in seconds and many of us do not even realize it.

How we show up is a choice we must make every day. How we "face" the world head on requires an intentional act of being present. Even when we do not feel like it, even if we do not feel well, even when all we want to do is lay in bed and block the world out. We all have those days, but what is important is to give ourselves grace because being an adult is not easy. In the current environment of technology, the first moment of interaction with someone else might be the only opportunity to communicate and the question is how do you want the other person or group to receive you? What are you doing to open the line of communication and build the bridge of understanding?

Many of our initial communication interactions today use technology—email, text, emoji, or meme—creating an unspoken barrier blocking us from having a real communication interaction. I can hear folks now; those are legitimate ways to communicate with someone! My question for those folks is simple. Then why do so many people find it so hard to communicate with people directly, one-on-one, without technology? Why is there always confusion and misunderstanding? I want you to really think about it. Can you remember the best moments with family, a loved one or a friend, talking or cracking jokes or sharing a moment with a loved one? Nothing beats face-to-face interaction.

It is simple; we are humans, with different experiences, knowledge, and emotions, who all need human interaction. It sounds cliché but everyone needs someone. Some people thrive in solitude, but most do not. Using technology as your only means of communication is bound to cause disconnection, misunderstanding, and confusion. Your thoughts are yours alone. You may think you are clear in your message, but the other person cannot read your thoughts. They may or may not be able to see your body language. The other person is left to their own interpretation of your message.

Be mindful that people are emotional beings and will create their own stories to rationalize their own actions or based on their past experiences. Haven't you heard people say, "He was yelling at me in the email!" or "She had an attitude in her email." First, I did not know letters or words had emotions; second, did you ask or are you assuming the other persons' intentions? The words on the screen are just that—words. It is the reader's decision on how to interpret the words. Whether you like it or not people are developing their own opinion of what they first see. They are going to develop their own story or message to what they see based on their own individual experiences or knowledge and ideas.

It is a natural occurrence for people to develop their own interpretation. We all do it. We will always rely on what we know and what is familiar. What is tied to the message? What is the goal? What will be your first step towards establishing communication with others? This is the first step in developing your dance.

This is true of any task you must do, whether it is work or your personal life. Have you ever wondered why some people successfully execute multiple tasks with ease, while others seem unable to execute one task? A reminder that everyone is different, but being different does not mean it is bad. What it does mean is that you must be fully committed to the process of effective communications to build relationships that matter. Learning the steps to effective communication is much like creating your own unique dance—it requires intention, practice, and rhythm. Just as a dance is designed from individual movements that flow together, effective communication is developed through mastering key techniques. When these techniques are consistently applied, they create an environment where meaningful and successful interactions with others can take place.

Music plays an integral part in how well we dance with others. Many of us listen to music, but the question is what is the song that is playing in your head? What type of music moves you? When I lead a training session, I make a point to shake things up, especially after lunch, when energy tends to dip. That is when I like to toss in something completely unexpected to re-engage the room. One of my favorite ways to do this is by asking, "If you could pick a song to describe your life right now, what would it be?" It is such a profound question that really stops most people in their tracks. It catches people off guard in the best way and opens the door to connection, reflection, and a few good laughs. Because music is that powerful. Different songs move us in different ways because our musical preferences are shaped by our personal experiences, ideas, and influences. There are songs that make us snap our fingers, tap our feet, or move us to dance. As individuals, our own thoughts, mixed in with traditions and influences directly or indirectly affect our choices of music, but remember what moves one, does not always move another. What appeals to one person may not affect another the same way.

Everywhere throughout the world, there are sounds that come together to make music and these same sounds can affect others in ways we never imagined. How many of us rarely listen to reggae, yet start dancing to it whenever we are on vacation? Music could represent a happy or a sad memory, a tragic event or a monumental one, like a wedding or a big win. It can help cheer people on or become the soundtrack of a protest! It conjures up special moments in history that cross borders, cultures, languages, or generations that can share the same song, but each have a different meaning for the listener.

My best friend Lisa and I went to Puerto Rico to celebrate my birthday, a girl's weekend. It was our opportunity to reconnect, gossip, chat, and enjoy our friendship. A friendship that has spanned 40+ years. We went to a local bar with other friends from the island. It was one of those spots only a local would know. A great little spot that was open air, great island vibes, music playing on all the screens, and a jukebox. It was one of those places that you never forget and makes your vacation memorable.

While sitting together, ordering drinks, and snacks, a video screen plays a song that was so infectious that people started dancing, tapping their feet, or moving their heads to the beat. Lisa and I had never heard the song before, but we liked it. For context, my girlfriend is not Spanish and not an American, but she liked the song. I did have to translate the Spanish words for her to understand the song and its meaning. A perfect example is that music, like dance, crosses all boundaries. Music is a unifier, a connector that sets the stage for relationships to grow.

When we each landed in our respective homes, Lisa in Bermuda and I in New York, that song served as a reminder of our girl's weekend. Within the month, the song became the hottest song that summer and the most streamed song in the world. It set records and achieved unprecedented global music success. The funny thing was that the song was completely in Spanish with a mix of music genres, like reggaeton and rap, but then a big pop star joined in on a remix, singing his part in English, taking the song to a whole other level—making people dance to the same song regardless of language, location, or country.

That is what music does; it allows you to add your style to your dance steps. When we communicate with others, we are constantly faced with different people, challenging situations, short timelines, and unexpected "fires." We must find the right "dance" needed for the relationship and the situation, whether work or personal, we are all faced with the challenge of how do we "dance" or effectively communicate with someone else?

Now step left, step right with a slow rhythm...
Step 1, Step 2... Slow, slow. Step 1... Step 2... Slow, slow.

III. THE SOLOIST

When it comes to dancing, there are a variety of categories that you will need to tap into when effectively communicating. In this chapter, we will discuss one of the hardest and most courageous categories to be in. The soloist or solo dancer. Being a solo dancer is like being a solo communicator—graceful, independent, and fully in control of your own rhythm. The freedom to make quick decisions allows you to pivot instinctively, respond to the music of the situation, and express your vision without compromise.

A solo dancer practices every day, every step, they design every detail, normally to one song. It takes commitment, dedication, and a sense of confidence in what you are doing. This might be the easiest place to be or the worst because it is all about you. You can do what you want, dance any way you like, but this also means you are solely responsible for the dance and outcome. You do not have to worry about anyone else because there is no one else but you. No one is challenging your dance, ideas, or your style.

This autonomy can be powerful, especially when time is limited and direction is crucial. However, dancing alone also means you bear the full weight of the performance. There is no one to catch you if you stumble; there is no one to step in to help or support. Without a willingness to collaborate, your solo act can become isolating, blind to new choreography, and the enriching influence of others. Just as dance flourishes in duet or ensemble, communication thrives when voices move together, even if one leads the step.

It also means the spotlight is on you. It is also one of the scariest places to be, because it does not matter if you are nervous or not, comfortable, or uncomfortable, at the end of the day you are the one in the spotlight. Have you ever witnessed someone speaking to a large group of people and wondering how they do it? How do they feel comfortable being the center of attention, everyone is watching them perform? This is a reality for leaders and a situation all future leaders will face. You might be a community leader, a leader in your church, your office, or in your home, whatever the stage, everyone is looking to you for leadership, guidance for everything. It is a scary spot to be in, been there, done that.

Standing on your own, going against what is the norm, the fear of failing, of not being able to deliver is the scariest spot you will ever face, but the flipside is that it will be one of the most fulfilling and rewarding experiences you will have ever had.

All of us have suffered a moment of doubt, where we doubt ourselves, our skills— where the "imposter syndrome" monster kicks in. Imposter syndrome is that inner voice whispering that you are not good enough, even when all evidence points to the contrary. It can keep you stuck—doubting your abilities, second-guessing your success. But the key to overcoming it is not perfection; it is momentum. Whether you are leaping ahead, taking a sidestep, or inching forward one shaky step at a time, progress is power. Each move, no matter the direction, chips away at doubt and builds confidence. The point is not to arrive; it is to keep going.

I can now laugh about my first freezing experience. I genuinely thought I was going to have my first panic attack or nervous breakdown. I share this because I want you to understand that it is normal to be nervous. I see nerves as a barometer of how much I care about my work, its importance, or the relationship. Those thoughts of: You do not belong here; they will not listen to you; you are not supposed to be here because you are too different, too young, a woman, you are Latina... blah, blah, blah. It is easy to come up with excuses as to why you can't do something. So, tell me, why the heck not? What's the absolute worst thing that can happen? You stutter? You trip over a word, your feet? You turn red? Big deal. Join the club! Public speaking makes a lot of people uncomfortable, but honestly, what's the real risk? The world won't end. You'll survive. And next time, you'll be even stronger. The truth? You're braver than you think. Every time you dare to try, you level up.

Not too long ago, I was speaking at a large university in Texas. By this time, I am super comfortable with speaking to large crowds. I thrive on it. But something happened, I fell down the stairs in front of everyone. I was mortified! I wanted to hide, but that was not an option. I tried to ask my spouse to help me move away from the audience, but I was stopped mid-sentence by the police captain who said, "Absolutely not, you sit there until the ambulance comes." Ugh, if I could have made myself disappear, I would have. There I was—surrounded by students, teachers, school leaders, parents, and generous sponsors. The room was buzzing with pride and possibility. And then... life threw me a plot twist.

An ambulance and a police escort. Yes, you read that right, a police escort. I actually asked them, half-joking, is there something you're not telling me? Because I've never had a police escort before—am I dying or something? Looking back, I can laugh about it now, but at that moment, it was no joke. I had fractured my foot—not in one, not in two, but in three places. Classic me. I don't do anything halfway; I go full throttle, even when I'm falling (quite literally) flat on my face.

And let's add some flair to this dance of chaos: it all happened in Texas. Which meant I had to go back to New York—with a shattered foot, a suitcase full of pain, and pride that had taken a bit of a tumble too. Not exactly a trip for the faint of heart. But what were my options? I could've cried about it, sulked, thrown a pity party. Or I could do what I always do—accept the moment, find the lesson, and move forward with style. Now, this wild detour has become one of my favorite stories about resilience, humor, and unexpected grace.

Two wonderful and unexpected things came out of this embarrassing event. The first was the situation confirmed the importance of building relationships and empowering others. I had three volunteers/colleagues support the event. This was the first time we were together. Once I fell, the event still had to go on. There were community leaders and representatives there, in addition to all the others. Because we had prepared and discussed the agenda, they knew what was going on and they were flexible and stepped in. No, they stepped up and took the event over. The second thing was the unexpected appreciation from others.

I never do anything for praise, but it sure does feel good when others acknowledge or express their gratitude.

After the whole fiasco, I asked one of the event directors why there was such an elaborate escort and response, he looked me straight in the eye and said, "Because you made this event happen. You took the time to meet with the students and their parents. No one else has ever come to this school representing the federal government, showing them what is possible. We appreciate you."

That moment—that sincere gratitude—meant everything. So, do I really care about the fall? Absolutely not! That fractured foot came with something far more valuable: stronger relationships with my colleagues and a heartfelt "thank you" from a community I was honored to serve.

When you are faced with a challenge, you must meet it like a dancer stepping onto an unfamiliar stage—head held high, heart open, and ready to move with purpose, which is easier said than done. We all have fears, every single one of us, but how we react is where the leaders rise. Even if the music is unexpected or the steps are unclear, you face it with confidence, trusting your foundation, and adjusting with grace.

Imagine a solo dancer on a dimly lit stage—spotlight fixed, silence pressing in, the audience unseen but deeply felt. Each movement, every breath, is a quiet act of courage. Facing your fears is much like this—stepping into the light alone, vulnerable, and exposed. There is no partner to lean on, no chorus to hide behind. It's you, your fear, and the rhythm of your own heartbeat. But the dance must begin. Like fear, the first step is the hardest—the moment when uncertainty starts to creep in—yet, with every step, every pose propels you into motion. Motion creates momentum, and with each step your fear slowly transforms into a dance.

Being a solo dancer is a powerful metaphor for the experience of communicating alone; you must learn to face your fears. Act on it! Learn to assess your audience. Ask yourself, what is your goal for the interaction? Did you assess the situation? What are the options? What hasn't worked for the audience? What steps have been taken in preparation for the interaction? What steps do we know? Change is never easy and for some can cause outright anxiety. I am one of those rare birds that likes change. I like learning new things, seeing new things, and experiencing new things.

Challenges, too, are choreographed into the routine—not obstacles to halt you but pivots that demand grace and resilience. A stumble does not end the performance; you learn to make it part of your performance. Remember the story of the dance performance when the music would not play? We stepped up and made the "issue" part of the dance routine. We were confident in our abilities to perform; we practiced and practiced. We knew the routine, but our teacher always told us to keep moving. If you make a mistake, just keep moving because the audience doesn't know if it was part of the routine or not. The solo dancer learns to bend without breaking, to recover without shame. Each turn and leap represents persistence, shaped not by perfection but by adaptation. It is through repetition and reflection that balance is found-onstage and in life. When challenges arise, we are called not to avoid them but to incorporate them into our rhythm, adjusting the steps as you go.

As leaders you will often be required to make decisions that may not always be welcomed by the team. It requires you to take the lead and perform alone, until the team has mastered the tasks and are working collectively to get the job done. Effective communication is the dancer's ability to speak without words. The audience may not hear a voice or a sound, but they feel the story—the intention behind each motion. Just as the soloist must project meaning through their body, we communicate not only with what we say, but with how we say it. Honesty in gesture builds trust, just as clarity and presence in our conversations foster connection. Like dance, effective communication requires listening—to music, to silence, to the unspoken emotions of others—and responding with empathy and authenticity. In this way, even when we dance alone, we never truly dance in isolation.

It is a one-sided performance and never a comfortable spot to be in, but crucial to your own personal and professional growth. Understand as a leader, you will all have to perform alone—at work, at home—because it is your ability to adapt to the situation at hand that is your key to success.

IV. DUETS

In duet-style dancing, each person brings their own movement, their own vocabulary, their own ideas. No two dancers are the same, but when they are attuned to each other, something wonderful happens. Each dancer is still their own individual self but through their commitment to execute they somehow bridged the language of communication. The same is true in conversation.

Communicating one-on-one is much like performing a duet in a dance routine, it requires mutual awareness and rhythm, but most importantly trust. Duet-style interactions, whether in dance or dialogue, carry a unique intensity. With only two people involved, there is no room to hide behind a group or blend into the background. It is very much like dance; you take cues from each other, you match energy, you fall into rhythm. And just like in dance, especially a duet, this form of interaction demands presence, vulnerability, and deep mutual awareness. We may have different styles, motivations, or comfort zones, but we often share more common ground than we expect—a desire to be heard, understood, and respected.

Sometimes you might see a pair of people dancing like the famous Fred Astaire and Ginger Rogers, or a group of people and wonder how they do it? How do they keep the synchronization so perfect? Practice. How do they know when to step together? Practice. How do they predict their partners' next move? Practice. You know the adage "practice makes perfect?" However, that is just a piece of the puzzle. The most vital piece to the interaction is the commitment to executing the dance together to reach the goal.

In a duet, each dancer brings their own unique energy and style, yet both must move in unison for the performance. Not just unison, but they must move in harmony and passion for the performance to succeed. This requires each dancer to set aside their personal feelings and opinions to ensure that the performance is cohesive and the dancers perform as one. Even if you don't like the other person. This isn't personal, you both have a job to do.

When the duet is with a superior or involves a personal matter, the stakes can feel higher. You feel exposed, like the spotlight is on you and there is no safety net. This is where your ego must take a back seat. You can't lead and listen at the same time. Checking your ego means allowing space for the other person's perspective and being open to shifts in direction. You can't force a connection; they happen naturally over time and are found in each individual moment.

To execute a two-person interaction effectively, start by grounding yourself. Listen not just for words, but for tone, posture, and the space between thoughts. Observe and mirror their energy when appropriate for opportunities for alignment. This is done through asking questions. Asking the right questions in a two-person interaction is like setting the rhythm in a duet; it helps guide the flow, builds connection, and opens the door for deeper understanding. The right question doesn't just show that you're listening, it proves you're engaged, curious, and respectful of the other person's perspective.

In effective one-on-one communication, success comes when both of you are in sync with one another. Their cues show they're truly tuned in, listening closely and replying with clear intent. The other person's cues are everything—subtle shifts that show they're engaged, listening with intention, and responding with deliberate care. It is not just about movement, it is about meaning. You cannot dance a duet by focusing only on your steps; you must also feel the presence and flow of your partner. The same is true in communication. In an intimate exchange, especially one with high stakes or emotions, good questions help clear the air. It helps clarify the goals of the conversation and when done correctly it will help identify what is unsaid. They invite reflection instead of defense, and they signal that you are not just waiting for your turn to speak; you are creating space for authentic dialogue.

A well-placed question can de-escalate tension, clarify confusion, and even shift power dynamics to make the interaction feel more collaborative. For example, instead of stating, "We need to fix this," ask, "What do you think would be the best way forward?" It shifts the tone from pointing the finger to a partnership. Think of questions as spotlights: they can illuminate what matters most, help both see more clearly, and often reveal a path that was not visible before. Success comes from truly engaging with the other person, not just speaking your mind, but also being open to receiving the other person's ideas.

A few tips to keep your steps in sync:

- *Start with Intention*: Like dance partners meeting at center stage, they begin with a shared purpose. What are we here to accomplish? What is the end goal?

- *Awareness:* Pay attention to how the other person moves. Do they need more space, time, affirmation, or redirection? Remember everyone processes information differently. Grant the space for someone else to process at their own speed.

- *Lead, Support, Follow*: Lead when needed, support when appropriate, and follow when required. Don't be afraid to take the initiative but recognize when the moment calls for stepping back. Just like in a dance, each individual will have steps to follow.

- *Bow*: As dancers close a performance, applause will be received with a bow; end the conversation with clarity, appreciation, or a mutual understanding of what comes next.

Mastering the duet is not about dominance or submission, it's about creating something meaningful together in real time. There will always be a dance of give and take when in a duet. It is a dance that can easily be influenced by outside factors: personality, authority, power, attitude, cultures, experiences, etc.

When your dance partner has a different personality or style—maybe they're more reserved, while you're more expressive—it doesn't mean you can't perform together. It means you both must learn to find common ground, to adapt and adjust. It is not a one-way process, both of you must commit to making the interaction work. In dance, this might mean changing a step, adjusting your posture to create a balance where you both shine. In communication, it means recognizing their preferred style— whether they're more analytical, need more time to process, are more emotional or assertive—and adjusting your approach.

Instead of overpowering, withdrawing, or becoming defensive, you work together to find what compliments you both. If your partner is more detail-oriented or cautious, you will need to slow down, seek clarity, and patience to foster greater understanding. This goes back to our first chapter about setting the stage.

Imagine communication through the eyes of a dancer. Before you step onto the floor, you have to recognize your own rhythm, what drives you, what throws you off, and what brings you into flow. That is recognizing what makes you tick. But dancing alone is not the goal. The real magic happens when you tune into your partner's tempo—what inspires them, challenges them, and moves them forward. That is figuring out what makes them tick.

In a duet, the magic lies not just in choreography, but in the connection. Great dancers do not just execute steps; they read each other, moment by moment, breath by breath, to deliver an exceptional performance. It is a silent dialogue of cues: a glance, a shift in weight, the subtle tightening of a hand, or an extended hand waiting for you to connect. It is the same in a conversation; when someone is attentive, their cues form an emotional rhythm. Their body language, facial expressions, and tone reveal whether they're with you in the moment. When they're actively listening and responding with intention, it feels like you are dancing in sync—two people creating meaning in real time.

A conversation is a duet around shared goals. As dancers, you both want to create a seamless, expressive performance. You want the audience to feel the dance. You want to touch the audience in a way that reaches the very core of who they are after each performance. In one-on-one communication, collaboration means aligning around a common purpose—whether it is solving a problem, making a decision, or building a relationship. This involves giving and receiving feedback, like dancers exchanging signals, adjusting along the way. This is how you build trust. When both individuals commit to communication as a shared effort, not a solo performance, their synergy elevates the outcome.

And just like in dance, if one partner stops paying attention or tries to dominate, the whole performance falls flat. That is why true duet-style communication requires humility, presence, and responsiveness. It is not about outshining the other person; it is about elevating each other. You do not need to have all the right moves. You just need to keep showing up, tuning in, and adjusting your steps. That is the real artistry of connection, dancing until you find the move that opens the doors of opportunity.

A successful duet depends on practice, respect, and being present. The more you work together, the more fluent your communication becomes—just like dancers who have practiced their steps and can anticipate each other's movements without speaking. Even when there are missteps, the goal is not perfection but connection. There is no such thing as perfect, and who wants to be perfect? Boring. I suffered (well, still suffer) from that awful disease of perfectionism but have learned not only to accept that life happens and that you cannot control everything. Being open to new ideas or thoughts can take you to heights you have never imagined. When you see communication as a dance—fluid, responsive, and shared—you become more equipped to engage in meaningful interactions, especially with those who move to a different beat. Dance through it all.

Add three steps, in quick rhythm... Step left, step right, step left. Add the quick step in place for a count of three. Slow, slow, quick, quick, quick.

V. ENSEMBLES

Communicating effectively with a group or team is like performing an ensemble dance—dynamic, multiple moving parts, and entirely dependent on mutual awareness. Each person brings a different rhythm, tempo, and movement style— shaped by their background, personality, and role. Some bring bold, radiant energy while others offer quiet precision behind the scenes, but each plays a vital role in the success of the entire performance. The art is in weaving all those unique energies into one cohesive performance. It doesn't mean everyone moves the same way; it means they move together. Like instruments in an orchestra or dancers in an ensemble, their impact lies not in sameness, but in the harmony they create together.

In group dance, dancers rely on awareness of each other's energy, timing, and positioning to avoid stepping on toes and keep the flow going. There is a constant changing of roles, steps, and positioning throughout a performance. One person signals the next move, someone else handles the transition, and the entire group keeps things moving smoothly, maintaining the flow for a successful result. When communication breaks down—just like in dance—you'll feel it in the missteps, awkward pauses, and people colliding (figuratively and literally).

Let's get ready to dance into a familiar scene, one many of

us have survived: the "voluntold" project. You know the type. A cross-functional initiative that comes from above with layers of complexity, multiple business units involved, and a room full of smart (or not so smart) people—each with their own processes, ideas, priorities, and personalities. On paper, it looks like a collaborative masterpiece. In reality? A standstill. No one wants to budge, and everyone insists their process is *the* process, their idea is the best idea. And you, lucky you, have just been dropped into this swirling storm with a polite smile and a deadline.

So, what do you do?

First step, don't talk—listen. I have learned that before jumping into action, I go quiet. I request everything: project reports, meeting notes, email summaries, whatever breadcrumbs are available—because you can't fix what you haven't studied. You would not join a dance mid-performance, without knowing the choreography. This is the same thing.

Next, I meet one-on-one. Not in a group, not in a high-pressure meeting, but individually, where honesty lives. I speak with each stakeholder and every lead to understand what is really going on beneath the turf wars and tension. Then I return to the basics, every time.

I start asking:

- What is the true goal of this project?

- Who is involved, and what do they care about?

- What outside pressures or variables are in play?

- What's the timeline, and how firm is the budget?

- Most importantly, what previous approaches have been attempted, and what were the reasons for their lack of success?

Because here is the truth: *you cannot build something new if you don't understand what already fell apart.* Jumping forward without that knowledge guarantees repeated missteps. When you start from curiosity instead of control, you begin to reconnect the rhythm and remind the group that progress isn't about winning—it's about weaving together the pieces that already exist.

In group communications, individuals must be self-aware, open to listening and sharing space, be mindful of the words you say, your body language, and how they affect the team dynamics. In an ensemble, just like in a group, there should not be one person who dominates over the others, no one voice should overshadow others in a collaboration. Yes, I know it is hard when you have leaders or individuals who will bully their way into the spotlight. It is not uncommon to encounter situations where a leader or another individual does not contribute to the execution of a project but takes full credit for the group's achievements. No recognition, no kudos, nothing. It is disheartening, but it is a lesson for you to keep in mind if your goal is to become a leader. Never, ever be one of those leaders who does not support their team. As a leader, your goal should always be to support, promote, and create more servant leaders, not egomaniacs. Yes, I said it. Egomaniacs.

In any ensemble, there will be different personalities, which is obvious. Dancers can be bold and expressive; others may be quiet and precise. In a group, team members have diverse communication styles—some are confident and loud, while others are more reserved and need time to process. A skilled choreographer creates space for each dancer to shine while still holding the group together. Just think about your family or your friends. Some you love, some you don't, but you are all individuals with your own style. Haven't you ever looked at a sibling, friend, or family member and wondered how you can be so different when you have had similar experiences?

To add more flair for drama, there may also be mini routines within the main choreography, sub-teams working on different tasks, or quieter voices navigating their own movements. For an ensemble to succeed, these mini performances must connect back to the central rhythm. Picture a dance troupe preparing for a major performance. Each dancer specializes in certain moves, yet they must align under a shared vision. That is project management in motion.

Just like a choreographer maps out a routine, the lead or manager sets the roadmap—the milestones, responsibilities, and outcomes. But execution depends on the team's ability to move as one while honoring each member's unique strengths. In any ensemble performance—on the stage or in the workplace— honoring each member's strengths is like spotlighting their signature move in a larger choreography. Everyone brings something unique to the performance. To respect these differences, start by observing each team member's natural rhythm—how they communicate, how they work, when they shine. Open conversations about strengths and preferences and resist the urge to mold everyone into the same steps. Instead, choreograph a routine where their individual talents not only fit, but enhance the collective flow.

Effective communicators do the same thing—acknowledging the individual styles and finding ways to create harmony within the team. This might mean taking extra steps to draw out quieter team members, setting boundaries for more dominant voices, or serving as a translator between styles to foster mutual understanding. When the team's strengths are recognized and integrated, the group moves as one—seamless, collaborative, and powerful. The true synergy happens when no one is out of place, everyone has a role, and every step matters.

Working with various levels of authority adds another layer in the group dance. There are leads and background dancers in choreography—just like there are managers, team leads, and support staff in a team setting. While the lead may serve as a guide for the group, the group's success depends on each person performing to the best of their ability. Communication must be respectful of the hierarchy but not confined by it. Like in dance, where cues can be passed subtly and power can shift in a routine, effective team communication allows for input from all levels, fostering an environment of shared responsibility and creative exchange.

Change—whether in choreography or team dynamics—can be disruptive, even paralyzing but can also be energizing. In dance, a change in music, a step, or formation requires adaptability and trust in your fellow dancers. In communication, change may mean new goals, leadership, or challenges. It's critical to keep the lines of communication open, to establish alignment, and to stay connected to the team's rhythm. Successful teams navigate change by staying focused and grounded in their shared purpose, just as dancers find their footing by returning to the beat. This is where music, like boundaries, helps keep the dancers and the team moving forward. A team lead may do that for the team, and music with its beats helps dancers get back on track.

Ultimately, collaboration is about moving as one while honoring everyone's contributions. It is about ensuring that all movements support the vision of the performance. When communication flows like a well-rehearsed group routine-coordinated, respectful, and intentional-goals are met more effectively, and the entire group shines.

When you step left, swing your hips left. Step right, swing your hips right.

VI. CHOREOGRAPHY (THE HOW)

You might ask, where or how do I even begin? Start by defining your own boundaries, goals, and negotiable points for the event. The first step in developing your communication strategy starts with you. What are you willing to accept? What do you want out of the event? What do you need to get out of this event? What are the steps you are willing to negotiate on? These fundamental questions apply whether you are a soloist, in a duet, or a group setting. Each step builds on the idea that just like dancing, communication is an intentional, practiced, and expressive act that requires commitment, self-awareness, rhythm, and connection.

I know, I know, I know, some of us have more rhythm than others but that does not mean you cannot find your rhythm so you can execute. Just like there are different dance styles, there are different communication styles.

Step 1: Find Your Rhythm – Self-awareness and Intent

Before stepping onto the dance floor, you know what your rhythm is—your style. Effective communication starts with self-awareness. It is important to identify your own communication style, understand your triggers, recognize your strengths, and the areas of opportunities you can expand on. Like a dancer knowing the timing and beat of the routine, you must be clear about your intent and message. Whether you are a soloist, in a duet, or in an ensemble, your ability to be self-aware of who you are, what is important to you, and what your values are aid in your journey. In solo settings, this is about internal clarity. In duets or groups, this awareness becomes the foundation of every interaction. Being clear about your intent and the message you wish to convey contributes to more effective interactions. If you are not clear on who you are and what your needs are, how do you expect to communicate with others?

Please, do not confuse what I am trying to convey. Every one of us has values that are part of the very core of who we are as individuals. These cores are embedded in who we are and are the hidden parts that form your foundation. You cannot leap from a weak foundation; you need to create a solid foundation to build from.

Step 2: Learn the Basic Steps – Core Communication Skills

Every dance, every routine you are about to make begins with basic steps. Basic steps that when combined create the bridge to communication. Before you can dance you must master the basics before you can improvise and adapt for growth in your communication style. Building foundational skills, like active listening, clear articulation, body language, and tone. These are the "basic steps." Without them, any communication—like any dance—can become awkward, misguided, or misunderstood.

Effective communication, much like a well rehearsed dance, relies on fundamental moves that never go out of style. So, let us get down to basics. The four core skills are: active listening, clear articulation, body language, and tone. They are the building blocks of every interaction and are essential steps that bring grace and cohesion to every exchange. They're simple in concept, but when practiced with intention, they can transform any conversation into a seamless duet or an ensemble masterpiece.

Imagine stepping into a duet or ensemble performance. Without listening to your partner's rhythm, how would you know when to move? Without clarity in your own steps, how would others know how to follow or respond? These core communication skills are the foundational steps of any effective interaction, just as basic footwork is essential to dance. There are various dance styles that are very structured and serve as the foundation for other styles. For example, when I used to study dance, the teacher made me start with ballet. I did not want to study ballet; I wanted to study jazz. However, the teacher explained that to study jazz, I needed to learn the basic structure of dance— posture, foot positions, etc. It was not my favorite time, because I thought it was too strict. Guess what, it was exactly what I needed to become a better dancer.

Active Listening

Active listening can be compared to following your dance partner's lead, cue awareness. It tells you when it is your turn, when to pause, and how to mirror what has been expressed. It keeps you present, flexible when planning your next move. It is the equivalent of locking eyes with your dance partner and staying in step. It's not just about hearing words; it's about tuning into meaning, intention, and emotion. Just as dancers must respond to subtle shifts in movement, communicators must be present enough to pick up on nuances, allowing space for others to feel seen and heard. It is the ability to listen to the other person without interruption, without responding. Just listen, emotions in check, waiting to respond. Give the other person your full attention.

Clear Articulation

Clear articulation is how you choreograph your message. It ensures your words hit their marks, just like precise steps land on a beat. When you express yourself with clarity, others don't need to guess your intent. They can follow your lead and move with you toward mutual understanding. It emulates precise foot placement; each word should be delivered with intention and clarity to avoid any confusion. It's not about using complex language but about using the right words with purpose.

Body Language

Body language in communication is considered the hidden factor and the largest part of communication. Most think it is the verbal part of communication that is most important, but it is not. Body language, the non-verbal part of communication and the hardest to master, is the largest unspoken factor. It fills the space between the words. A nod, an open stance, a forward lean—these are the extensions of your voice that tells others, "I'm with you." Body language is the equivalent of posture and form in dance; your stance, gestures, and eye contact either invite connection or create distance. In dance, tension in the frame can disrupt the partnership. In conversation, misaligned body language sends mixed signals.

Tone

And then there's tone, which sets the rhythm. It is the music of your message. Just as the mood of a song influences how you move, your tone conveys emotions and context beyond words. You can say the same words with warmth or with coldness, and the outcome changes completely. Tone sets the emotional rhythm. It tells your audience whether they can relax into the conversation or brace for impact. Like a song that stirs emotion, tone carries the weight of the connection.

These skills might be timeless, but are never truly mastered—they are practiced, refined, and rediscovered in every new interaction. When we communicate with the grace of a dancer—listening deeply, moving clearly, aligning our expressions—we do not just share information, we create connection. For example, a classical or instrumental slow tone when giving feedback is like dancing a waltz—slow, smooth, calming. While a loud, sharp tone in a disagreement can feel like a tango—sharp, aggressive, direct. Mastering these basics builds trust, ease, and flow, whether you are in conversation or on the dance floor.

When establishing the above basics, you need to do your due diligence. Your research on the other person's needs and wants will serve as opportunities where negotiations might be possible. This helps create a common ground and creates space to find the steps you are in sync with. Where do you need to adjust? Is this a solo part, a duet, or will it be best as an ensemble?

How many of us have gone on vacation and we start dancing

to all kinds of music we normally do not dance or listen to? I am sure all of us have experienced that moment of freedom where we allow ourselves to enjoy the moment. A perfect example is Reggae music. You may not normally listen to it back home, but you're on vacation, all your inhibitions are gone, you are open to trying something new, only to find out you love the sound, the way it makes you feel—the vibe, the tone. This is extremely important for you to be mindful of when dealing with others and trying to interact with others, you must maintain an open mind to something new. If you fail to keep an open mind when dealing with others it blocks you all from moving forward and meeting the goals. Just because people are different does not mean it is bad, it is simply different.

Step 3: Dancing with a Partner – Adaptability in Duets

Duets are tricky, because it is no longer just you, now you are faced with dancing with another person to meet the goals. In a duet, your steps must respond and coordinate with your partner's. When communicating one-on-one, practice mirroring, adapting, and responding to the other person. Like dancing in pairs, communication requires attentiveness, flexibility, and mutual respect. You can be the lead, or you may have to follow throughout the routine. Either position requires you to be able to reach verbal and non-verbal cues. You must adjust your pace, tone, and words to match the conversation. You must ensure you ask for clarity to make sure you are aligned.

Step 4: Practice with the Group – Synchronizing the Team

Dancing in an ensemble or group requires coordination, space awareness, and collaboration. In group settings, communication becomes more complex. Think of a dance troupe; each member has a role, and the success of the routine lies in the coordination and awareness of the collective movement. You must ensure that you are in the right place, that you are executing your part in alignment with the rest of the group. Here clarity, respect for different perspectives/voices, and facilitation skills are essential. This also requires you to be aware of the group dynamics, personalities, and energy.

Step 5: Rehearse, Rehearse, Rehearse – Practice and Feedback

During the previous chapter I mentioned the need to purposefully commit to the execution of the dance. Just as dancers commit to mastering a routine, effective communicators must purposefully rehearse the choreography of a conversation. It is not enough to understand the concept; you have to practice, listen, stumble, and learn from each interaction. The commitment isn't to be perfect or the best; it is to progress and build bridges of communication.

Repetition is what deepens the muscle memory and builds confidence. It strengthens your gestures and tone—not only in how you listen, respond, and recover when things go off script. Practicing in different situations helps you adapt your rhythm to any tempo, whether it's a calm one-to-one or a high-stakes group discussion.

Role-playing is especially powerful. It offers a rehearsal space free of consequences where you can experiment, adjust, and grow. And let's not forget, those handy little bricks we call phones? They double as rehearsal mirrors. Recording yourself may feel awkward at first, but it reveals what your tone, pace, and posture are saying before your words even land.

And then there's feedback—the dancer's mirror, the communicator's compass. Most people fear it and some avoid it altogether. Why? Because feedback nudges the ego, and growth rarely feels comfortable. But feedback is not criticism—it's a moment of calibration. It helps you fine-tune your timing, expand your range, and show up with more clarity and intention. Honest, constructive feedback—especially from trusted peers—is a gift. You want someone who can lovingly tell you when you've lost the beat, so you can adjust and return to the center.

In short, don't just talk. Practice. Don't just perform. Reflect. That's how you transform your communication from improvisation into artistry.

Step 6: Perform with Presence – Confidence and Expression

How many times have we witnessed an individual come into a room who just commands attention? I like to observe those individuals because you always learn something new. These instances show that holding a title does not necessarily indicate someone is a leader, as the person entering may or may not occupy the leadership role.

My dad once told me, "If you're uncomfortable or feel unsafe, seek out who's in charge." That simple piece of advice stuck with me—not just as a safety net, but as a mindset. It taught me the value of quickly reading a room, identifying authority, and adjusting my approach when necessary. Over time, that habit of observing before reacting has become second nature. It has helped me communicate with greater confidence, knowing when to speak up and when to listen. I am still working on strengthening the skill of staying calm. It is a hard one to master because we all have moments where someone or something triggers us and we "lose" control. In a world that moves fast and often throws curveballs, this early lesson has become my compass for staying grounded and effective.

During my time as a sales rep for a fashion company, I was assigned to a community where many store owners observed their religious traditions that created some very awkward moments. They refused to speak to me because I was not one of "them." I was a goy. Goy is a Yiddish word defined as someone who is non-Jewish. This particular shop owner would not speak to me at all. He would not even look in my direction. He would not interact with me simply because I was a woman and goy, but I had to get the order. I left the store angry and shocked. I needed to figure out how I was going to get the order AND get my emotions in check because I needed my job. I noticed a young man standing in front of another store location and asked if he would be interested in making a quick buck. I explained the situation and the young man went into the store and got me a huge order. It was worth every penny!

This is what I call my secret move—flexibility. In the choreography of communication, flexibility is your secret dance move, the one that keeps you grounded, yet agile when the tempo suddenly shifts. Difficult conversations are like improvised sequences in a dance; even if you've rehearsed your lines, the other person may lead with unexpected energy or emotion. That is where flexibility becomes essential—not just bending your stance but adjusting with purpose and poise to keep the flow going to reach the end.

Think of it like a dancer responding to a partner who missteps.

Instead of freezing or correcting harshly, a skilled dancer breathes through it, redirects, and finds a new groove—all while making it look seamless. In communication, that same grace shows up as listening, staying present, and knowing when to soften your tone or reframe your message. Flexibility allows space for emotion without letting it hijack clarity. It makes you responsive, not reactive.

Flexibility also means knowing that you do not have to finish the dance exactly the way you started it. You can shift direction mid-step, pause to reground, or even invite the other person to lead for a moment. It is not about losing control—it is about co-creating a rhythm that both people can move to. That is how hard conversations become breakthrough moments when you trade rigid choreography for intuitive connection.

Once you have practiced, know your message and deliver it with authenticity and your full attention. Effective communication is not just about words; it is about connection and being genuine. Whether you are solo, in a duet, or a group let your presence speak. Use your time wisely and pause intentionally. Express enthusiasm for the little things because they matter; make sure you have made eye contact and always engage with your audience.

Step 7: Improvise When Needed – Flexibility and Emotional Intelligence

What does improvisation mean? Improvisation is the distinct ability to do something without previous preparation, like what happened with that dance routine and the music didn't start and we were all on stage with the deer in headlights look. It took one of us to improvise and we all stepped up until the music started. Improvisation.

Whether in a communication exchange or a dance performance, flexibility and emotional intelligence are the unseen forces that shape the outcome. They are the twin pillars that make improvisation not just possible, but powerful. Emotional intelligence, at its core, is the ability to recognize, understand, and manage your own emotions while also being tuned in to the emotions of others. It is the inner compass that guides us and impacts how we respond—not just react—especially in moments of uncertainty or tension.

Flexibility is the body and mind's willingness to shift—direction, tone, posture, even intention—without losing balance or purpose. In dance, a performer may need to adjust mid-movement when a partner falters or if the music changes. Those who can adapt gracefully, without panicking, keep the rhythm going. The same holds true in conversation—flexible communicators don't cling to a script; they respond to the unfolding emotional landscape.

Sometimes the best moves are the ones we stumble upon. For example, I grew up in the era of breakdancing or breaking. When it first came out in the 70's in Da Bronx, yes, Da Bronx. It was frowned upon; some said it wasn't "real" dancing. It emerged as part of the hip-hop culture and was developed by the African American and Latino youth of the South Bronx. It was a direct result of the new hip-hop sound and still is one of the most acrobatic and creative dance forms around. Have you seen these dancers? I am in awe of their flexibility, their creativity, the moves they come up with—amazing. I may be a little biased since I am from NY, but, even when I was young and able, I still could not do it. I was not that fearless; the thought of me falling or hurting myself was a hard no. It slowly grew and started entering mainstream America. Breaking made appearances in movies like *Flashdance* (1983), *Breakin'* (1984) and *You Got Served* (2004). Breakdancing has continued to evolve and spread globally recognized as an art form and sport with its debut in the 2024 Olympics. Anything is possible but understand, it was not without controversy. The press and people came out with negative rhetoric around the hip-hop culture and breakdancing. Negativity is a common human reaction to something that is new or different.

Together, emotional intelligence and flexibility become part of your communications toolkit. Imagine entering a difficult conversation where someone's tone suddenly hardens. A rigid response might escalate the tension. But a communicator with emotional awareness senses the shift and, with flexibility, checks their own tone, body language, and adjusts their point to match the moment. Just like a dancer adjusting mid-performance, they maintain connection and flow without missing a beat.

It is fascinating how the human instinct often defaults to resistance when faced with something unfamiliar. This natural negative reaction—the quick surge of doubt, discomfort, or even fear—isn't a flaw in our character; it is a deeply rooted survival mechanism. The whole fight, flight, or freeze response is a natural reaction we all have. Our brains are wired to protect us, and anything unknown is viewed as a threat, whether it's a new idea, a different culture, or a shift in routine. But here is the truth, in modern life, many of the "threats" we encounter are not predators—they're just change showing up in disguise.

And so, the question is: *Why? Why are we so afraid of something new or different?* Part of the answer lies in the stories we tell ourselves.

Anything new often challenges our sense of control, identity, or certainty. It pushes us out of the familiar choreography of our days and into unfamiliar steps. But what if, instead of resisting the new, we became curious about it? We open our minds to something new without fear. Imagine if we adjust our attitudes, our perspectives, and seek to understand instead of attack? I can only imagine the positive outcomes that could happen if we paused before reacting.

In moments of challenge—when tension rises or opinions clash—we're presented with a choice: retreat into old patterns or *step toward growth*. These difficult interactions are not roadblocks; they are rehearsals. Each one teaches us to listen more deeply, express ourselves more clearly, and adapt with more grace. Over time, these moments become the very training ground where stronger communication is formed. When we lean into discomfort with openness, we do more than just grow our skillset—we prepare ourselves for transformation. We become more agile, empathetic, and resilient. We stop dancing the same solo and start learning the steps of connection, even across differences.

So, maybe the next time fear arises, we pause and ask: *What is this moment here to teach me?* That question, like a new rhythm, could be the start of a very different dance.

These skills are vital because communication, like dance, is a live performance—no two moments are exactly the same. And in the spaces where choreography gives way to instinct, it's emotional intelligence and flexibility that allow us to move with integrity, poise, and presence.

Step 8: Assess and Adjust – Continuous Growth

Even the best dancers review their own performances. Just like dancers and athletes, effective communications must regularly assess and adjust their skills to improve their performance. Dancers often watch recordings of their routines, analyzing posture, position, timing, and coordination. Athletes do the same thing, they study game footage to find the strengths, weaknesses, and strategic opportunities of the other team. They review their competitors' moves or plays the other athlete or team is known for. They also review their competitors to learn new techniques and anticipate challenges to stay ahead.

After every communication "performance," you should review what went well and what did not. Growth comes from taking the time to assess and adjust, not perfection. Like reviewing a recording of a dance routine, you are looking for areas to improve to help refine your own style, prevent mistakes, and perform at your highest level. This continuous cycle of assessment helps you refine your moves, your skills. The goal is always to put your best "foot" forward.

Like in communication, evaluating how you engage with others—listening, responding, interpreting the non-verbal cues—and learning from others sharpens your ability to connect and adapt in different scenarios. Growth comes from not just doing, but studying, learning, and evolving. When I worked for a major financial institution, a colleague asked me how I was able to "move" and connect in any room of people, no matter who the group of people were or where. She was amazed that wherever I was, whatever the situation, I was able to adjust and connect. I contribute this to my own personal growth as an individual and professional. Even if I was afraid, I would step into any situation with authenticity and my 100% attention. I wanted everyone to know I was here and committed to this interaction. Sometimes it had positive results, and there were also times it went unbelievably badly. So bad that I lost control of my emotions, which threw me off my routine.

Never empower anyone to have control over you. When you allow someone to "make" you angry or lose control you empower them to have control over you. Only you can allow yourself to lose control, only you can allow someone to hurt your feelings, only you can stop the negative rhetoric in your head. This is not easy. It is a hard lesson to master. Even today, there are times when someone does something that sends you over the edge and I have to remind myself I do not look good in orange.

When developing your personal communication—or dance—style, it all begins with mastering the fundamentals. Just like in dance, where learning the basic steps gives you the confidence to improvise, strong communicators start by grounding themselves in the essentials.

Think of the *who, what, where, when, why,* and *how* as your fundamental or foundational steps. These questions are the anchors that help you stay balanced no matter the tempo or complexity of the interaction. They guide your awareness of context, your intent, and your audience—much like a dancer who adapts to the music, the partner, and the space.

In real life or at work, these basics show up in tangible ways:

- **Who** are you speaking with? Adjusting your tone and message based on your partner ensures better connection—whether it's a teammate, a supervisor, or a client.

- **What** is the message? Being clear on what you want to express prevents missteps and keeps everyone in rhythm.

- **Where** is the conversation taking place? The setting matters—are you on stage in a meeting, or behind the scenes in a one-on-one?

- **When** is the right time to engage? Timing, like pacing in a dance, affects how your message lands.

- **Why** are you communicating? Purpose gives direction, just like a dancer's intention gives meaning to movement.

- **How** will you express yourself? Your style—whether assertive, empathetic, playful, or direct—adds personality to your performance.

Once you have mastered these basics, you can begin to add your unique flair. That is where the artistry comes in—reading the room like a dance floor, adapting your "choreography" mid-conversation, and leading or following as the situation calls for. This flexibility transforms everyday exchanges into meaningful and memorable connections.

As a dancer, you would take the time to identify who is going to be your partner or partners? What genre of music do you want to use? Where is this dance going to take place? When will this happen? Why are you doing this dance? How much time do you have before the actual performance and how do you plan to carry it all out? Every situation is going to be different. You must learn the importance of flexibility and learn to grow, adapt, adjust, and add your own flair. As I mentioned earlier, we are all different and as we grow and learn more, we are open to adopting new steps, adjusting, and making additions to customizing our own dance—it is your style. This is what works for you and may not work for everyone, which is 100% acceptable. This is a critical step in your growth process because you must find steps that feel comfortable for you to be able to add more to your dance moves. Set the stage.

Have you attended a wedding or birthday party where someone gets on the dance floor and starts dancing the Electric Slide? You can see all the "old heads" getting on the dance floor and then others decide to join in because it looks so much fun. Then the more experienced dancers start to add their own flair to the steps. They have mastered the basics to a point that it becomes second nature but then they add a twist to a step, a dip instead of a foot tap; still the same dance, but now they have taken it further. That is the phenomena around line dancing or group dancing—anyone can try. It allows everyone to take part whether you are an experienced dancer or not; whether you know the dance or not, the goal is not to be perfect at it, the goal is to have fun! Lots of fun!

In any relationship or communication event you must be intentional in your efforts. Whether it is a miscommunication, a conflict, a shift in dynamics, or a complete breakdown of understanding, real life rarely follows the perfect script we rehearsed. We all want to perform our best in any situation, whatever it is. We are all faced with two choices at every pivotal moment in time—positive or negative.

These moments are the true tests of communication, not when everything runs smoothly, but when things fall out of sync. Like in dance, where one misstep or change in formation can ripple through the entire performance, a disruption in communication can cause confusion, tension, and frustration. But just as an experienced dancer adapts mid-performance, resets, and continues with grace, effective communicators learn to pause, assess, and recalibrate their message and approach.

It is in these unpredictable, unscripted moments that our communication skills are refined, mastered. The "wrench" the world throws is not always a setback; it is often an opportunity to gain experience, to strengthen your resilience, and to deepen your understanding of others. We are reminded that communication is not a fixed routine; it is a living, breathing dance that requires constant awareness, flexibility, and a willingness to keep moving forward—even when the music does not start or changes unexpectedly. Just as dancers must listen for the beat and stay present in each count, communicators must be attentive, intentional, and aware of timing. Rushing ahead or falling behind breaks the connection. Patience is required.

As a dancer must know their foundational steps before stepping out onto the stage, effective communication begins with understanding your own core skills. These fundamentals— like active listening, clear articulation, proper tone, and awareness of body language—are basic steps. Before a dancer can perform a complex routine, they must first master the basic balance, posture, timing, and, most important, control. A dancer must always master control of their body and need to be aware of their abilities, strengths, and their own limitations. Before you enter a meaningful conversation, especially in a high-stakes or emotionally charged situation, you need a solid command of your communication skills. Without this foundation, interactions become unsteady, just like a dance falls apart when the rhythm is off.

When you know your strengths—whether it is your ability to empathize, clarify ideas, ask thoughtful questions, or remain calm under pressure—you bring confidence and clarity into every interaction. These are your practiced movements, the muscle memory you rely on when the unexpected happens. In dance, when the music shifts or your partner forgets a move, your grasp of the foundational steps allows you to recover gracefully. In communication, when someone reacts emotionally, misunderstands your intent, or details the discussion, your solid foundation helps you stay grounded and navigate the moment without losing connection.

A solid foundation allows for creativity and flexibility. Once a dancer has mastered the fundamentals, they can improvise, add flair, and adapt to new styles. The same is true of communication—when you are confident in the basics, you can shift your approach to suit different personalities, cultures, or group dynamics. You can build rapport, negotiate, resolve conflict, or inspire collaboration because you are not scrambling to remember what to do—you already know. Your base is strong, and from there, you can expand, evolve, and rise to meet the moment, no matter how the rhythm of the conversation changes.

If you do not take time to prepare or practice, you risk repeating the same missteps, and find yourself standing in the aftermath wondering, *What just happened?* Growth is rooted in intention. Every opportunity, whether it is your first time in a leadership role, meeting someone new, or joining a team, is an opportunity to learn, evolve, and refine—not rewind. That is where those basic skills become part of every aspect of your life.

Truly understanding those basic or foundational questions means being willing to turn them inward, asking them of yourself in every situation, not just of others. The simple, grounding inquiries—*Who? What? Where? When? Why? How?*—are not just for interviews or icebreakers. They are your internal compass. They're essential checkpoints, guiding you toward clarity, purpose, and alignment in your decisions, interactions, and leadership presence. Like any dancer who returns to the barre to maintain form, we must return to these questions to stay in sync with ourselves.

- **Who** am I becoming at this moment?

- **What** am I aiming to contribute or receive?

- **Where** am I in my journey—career-wise, emotionally, relationally?

- **When** is the right time to act or reflect?

- **Why** does this matter to me?

- **How** does this situation align with the person I want to be?

You wouldn't enter a dance floor with no sense of the beat, the space, or your partner. In the same way, stepping into real-life or professional dynamics without this self-awareness leaves you off-beat and uncertain. When you know your rhythm, you become a wise, adaptable, and intuitive communicator—someone others trust to lead and follow with grace.

Now, switch the dance to a relationship or a project you need to work on. Who is involved? What is the purpose or goal? Where is this going to take place? When does this need to happen or be completed by? Who are the players? Are there any external factors that could impede the success of the interaction? Why is it important? How do you plan to execute? Same questions, different scenarios. This type of dance does not happen only on dance floors, but in your everyday life, especially in the business world.

The truth is, we are all works in progress. Whether it's breaking a bad habit, learning a new skill, or reshaping a behavior that no longer serves us, we each carry the desire to grow. That drive—to refine, to evolve, to get back up when we stumble—it is what makes us beautifully, stubbornly human. Self-improvement is not a one-time performance; it is a lifelong rehearsal. Some days you crush the choreography; other days you trip over your own feet and wonder how you got so off-beat. But showing up, being willing to reflect, and doing the work—that's where real grace lies.

Dancing is the same way. We have all experienced a moment when we thought we were a hottie, fire, a baddie. You practiced a certain dance move; you practiced until you mastered the dance steps. You go to a party, check your nerves and get on the dance floor. You thought you were dancing well and then it happens, you see someone doing the same dance and realize, "I've been doing the dance the wrong way!"

You stop dead in your tracks. You freeze! You rush to get off the proverbial dance floor to avoid people looking or worse, laugh at you. Your heart stops, you feel paralyzed, you are about to freak out! Stop, take a breath and exhale. It could be a moment that traumatizes you, resulting in you never dancing again, or you can see what the other dancer is doing so you can learn. THIS IS NORMAL. I repeat, IT IS NORMAL. It is a normal reaction to want to stop and run away, or you can adjust your thought process and choose to stop, watch, and learn something new.

Have you ever wondered why some people don't care if they make a mistake while others are devastated? Why is it that some people can learn a new dance step right away and others must practice? There is a simple answer, we all process information differently and that is okay. It is better than okay, it is fabulous! That is what makes this crazy world great. Different people bring different rhythms—unique ideas, perspectives, dance steps, and ways of thinking. Each person adds their own flair to the floor, creating a mosaic of movement and meaning that wouldn't exist without their distinct presence.

We are all faced with choices, every single day. How you choose to dance in those situations is a choice that affects the outcome. In a dance, every movement follows a count—a structured rhythm, often in sets of 4-8 count, which guides the dancer through the entire dance. The count provides order, pacing, and flow, ensuring that the steps are in sync with the music and with others on the floor. Effective communication follows its own rhythm. There is a beginning where the intentions are set, a middle where thoughts are exchanged, and an end where dancers must listen for the beat and stay present in each count.

Communicators must be attentive, intentional, and aware of tone. When you honor the rhythm—whether in movement or in words—you create mutual understanding and a shared experience that leaves a lasting impression.

The first choice is the one where your ego kicks in. You do not want to feel vulnerable; you don't want anyone to laugh at you, so you opt not to make the first move. Your ego takes over and the fight or flight reaction is activated. It takes over, and your ability to think clearly overcomes your desire to learn, to be open to something new. That split second decision to run, instead of taking a pause to assess where you are, assessing the situation can either propel you to your success or your failure. Do you want to dance like everyone else, or do you want to be better? Do you want to be an average dancer or the principal dancer? What is your next move? Do you want to deliver an average performance, or do you want to deliver an outstanding one? Again, what is your next move?

The second move, or choice, is to check your learned behavior; stop, take a breath, and assess the situation. Are people really looking at you or laughing at you? Do you really care what others think; does it even matter? Is it useful to care what others think or is it better to take a different step? It is disempowering to worry about what others think. Making a conscious decision separates you from the average dancer. When you stop to watch the dancer(s) and the new steps, you are choosing **YOU**! You are choosing to learn, to grow, because you will always be the best project to work on. You opened your mind and the door to opportunities that you never knew existed. A great communicator and leader are always open to learning, wanting to grow, and improve. A great dancer is always practicing, studying other dancers, and learning new steps because a great dancer is always trying to be better to improve their performance.

You will always have to face different or tricky situations. You will always face situations that are beyond your control. I love to dance. I love music. It is something I like to do that brings me joy. Unfortunately, I had an accident that threatened my ability to walk, let alone dance. I twisted my ankle badly, which resulted in multiple surgeries, and complications that at one point threatened with an amputation. I freaked out. I called my doctor screaming, "I need to dance again." His response was, "Okay, but let's get you walking first." It was a long journey, multiple surgeries, wheelchair, walkers, canes until I could walk on my own.

I share this story because, with all the surgeries I had with my ankle, the result was a permanent limp. I was forced to face a situation I could never have imagined. I had to stop and assess my current situation. I had to reassess the shoes I wore, the way I walked, even the way I dressed. I had to consider what I could and could not do but I had to move. Moves that I have never had to make before. Steps that I have never learned or practiced. It was a situation I had no control of, but what I did have was choice. A choice to decide what was my next move, what was my next step.

The questions began. What do I have to change, adjust, or even say goodbye to? It was hard. I had to face my vanity, which I did not think I had. I loved dressing up and wearing sexy high heels. Not just because I was short, but because somehow, I was programmed to think I needed high heels to feel beautiful, sexy, more of a woman. I had to fight with my own thoughts, my own preconceptions, my own learned dance moves. All I knew was that I did not want to walk with a limp. I made a concerted effort to master the new steps. I was committed to learning how to walk with no or a minimal limp. I practiced my steps. I mean, I really practiced. I knew I was going to have to retrain my mind and body to learn something new and not fall back on my "old" way of doing things. I knew the consequences of my failure to practice would result in falling or hurting myself badly.

You see, it is easy to revert to your old steps. It is the most comfortable. It is always easier to do what is familiar. It is harder to be uncomfortable with a new situation and new dance. Your old dance steps are second nature to you. You practiced and executed those steps. You spent years developing and refining your style. But it's more serious than that, you must be committed to learning something new, intentionally practicing your new steps because if not you will always be in a situation where you repeat the old, get stuck in that repeat mode, and expect something different to occur knowing that it will not. You get stuck on repeat, dancing the same steps, and yet nothing happens. Wanting change and doing something to support that change is the deciding factor. You can make all the wishes you want, but until you purposefully make the effort to change and learn those new steps nothing will happen. Again, a choice.

The new steps require commitment on your part. First step, the desire to learn something new, but the most vital step is to execute that wish. Stop, assess, and adjust. I had to give up wearing high heels, but not all heels. I had to make an adjustment and lower my heel height. I cannot do all the dancing I used to, but I can still dance. I made a conscious choice to pivot and take a step forward. The goal is to always move forward.

Keep in mind any communication interaction, whether at work or in your personal life, you, a partner, or individuals will all play distinct roles. Sometimes we will be the lead "dancer" and sometimes we will play the supporting role. The key is to be flexible in every situation or relationship and to practice. Continuously practice your moves, where you can improve on? Ask yourself questions. What worked? What did not work? Why? How could I make it better next time? Assess and reassess. What worked in one situation may not work in another?

Freestyle music and dance is a way of dancing that was predominantly listened to in the Northeast during the 80's, where it started in NYC. It was a particularly good decade for new music genres. One of those new genres was Freestyle, a hybrid not only in dance, but also in sound. It combined a variety of rhythms— disco, Latin, and hip-hop. Dancers improvised dance moves right on the spot spontaneously moving to the music, within the situation or space you were in. It allowed you to develop your signature style, making your dance moves instantly recognizable. It was creative, imaginative, inventive, and original. Like communication, it is a series of movements, combined with basic dance steps, which offers an unlimited amount of flexibility for creativity to respond accordingly for that moment in time. Results can happen at once or overtime. Commit to communicating effectively. Stay consistent; do not let fear stop you from reaching your goals.

This is the point you want to aspire to. A point where you have mastered the basic dance moves, you have mastered your own style and are able to successfully maneuver in any situation you are faced with. You enter the dance slowly, use your basic moves, and as you assess the situation you can add moves. Add your own dance moves, your own style. It allows you the flexibility to communicate with anyone.

Consistency and kindness are the steady rhythm that makes any dance feel safe and inviting. When we choose to lead with grace—empowering others rather than pointing out their missteps—we create a space where trust can grow. It's like offering a gentle hand during a difficult turn, lending your strength instead of spotlighting another's stumble. In dance, as in life, it's not about perfect steps but about moving together with respect, patience, and encouragement. That kind of grace builds a bridge—one step, one beat at a time—toward lifelong relationships grounded in mutual support and understanding.

Now add the rhythm: slow, slow, quick, quick, quick...

1, 2... 1, 2... 1, 2, 3... 1, 2 ...1, 2 ... 1, 2, 3... Face forward, head straight, shoulders back, and SMILE!!!

VII. DANCE INTO YOUR OPPORTUNITY

Each interaction is an opportunity for you to perform. Each interaction is your opportunity to execute everything you have learned and practiced. When you see a performance, you are watching hours of practice, hours of designing, hours of rethinking and working through the steps to ensure everything coordinates.

You must realize that the steps you learn, the moves you make belong to you. Others will emulate you, try to be just like you, but no one can be YOU. You are special just the way you are. The only person you are in competition with is the old you. As you grow, learn new dance moves and improve you will want to be the best version of yourself. Learning to communicate is not something you can buy, not a possession someone can take from you. It is solely yours and only you can make the decision to look forward and dance your way into your own success.

You can only shape your story, achievements, and legacy; you play the leading role in this journey called life. Live your life, dance your way into every opportunity because every opportunity offers you the choice to show up. Choose wisely, live boldly, with audacity and authenticity. So, shine up those shoes and get to steppin'.

ABOUT THE AUTHOR

With a distinguished career spanning both public and private sectors, Migdalia Gonzalez is a master trainer, motivational speaker, author, and transformational coach dedicated to unlocking human potential. Known for expertise in personal development, leadership, and communications, she has empowered countless individuals and organizations to elevate their performance and embrace new opportunities.

As a sought-after speaker and trainer, Migdalia combines her extensive experience with a passion for helping others achieve their next level of success. Her fearless attitude and unwavering commitment to personal and professional growth create an environment where everyone can thrive. She believes in the power of dancing into opportunities and is devoted to guiding others on their transformative change with courage and enthusiasm.

Migdalia's unique approach blends practical insights with inspiring motivation, making her a catalyst for positive change. With a proven track record of leadership in various high-impact roles, Migdalia brings a wealth of knowledge and an unwavering dedication to her mission: transforming lives and inspiring excellence.